TAJ MAHAL

AGRA . FATEHPUR SIKRI

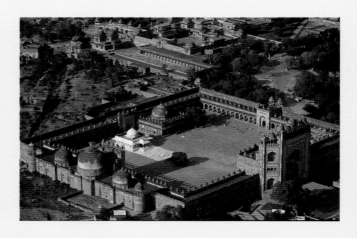

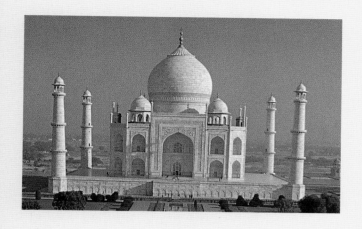

TAJ MAHAL
AGRA . FATEHPUR SIKRI

SHALINI SARAN

Lustre Press
·
Roli Books

Stories of the dazzling wealth of Hindustan had spread far beyond its borders. It was in quest of this wealth that Timur, better known as Tamerlane, and his ravaging hordes reached the banks of the river Indus in September of 1398. By December, Timur was enthroned in Delhi. For ten days he plundered, murdered and desecrated, and then left. In all he spent six months in Hindustan, leaving behind him untold devastation. He took with him elephants, a rarity in Central Asia, immeasurable quantities of booty, and perhaps most precious of all, the finest craftsmen to adorn his capital, Samarkand. It would never have occurred to him that in Hindustan, a little over a century later, a descendant of his would lay the foundation of one of the most splendid empires that ever existed.

This was the ornate Moghul Empire, ruled by such extraordinary men like Akbar, Jahangir and Shah Jahan. Shah Jahan—Emperor of the World—immortalized not only his beloved queen but himself and his whole dynasty by building that eloquent mausoleum, the Taj Mahal.

The founder of the Moghul Empire was Babur, "the Tiger." Born in the year 1483, he was the son of the Turki ruler of Ferghana, a kingdom that lay in the high steppes east of Samarkand. From his father's side Babur had the blood of Timur; from his mother's that of the Mongol, Ghengiz Khan, who, it is said, was "born with a clot of blood in his fist."

Babur was eleven years old when his father died, and at this tender age he found himself ruler of Ferghana. But he was not destined for a peaceful reign and for several years, he roamed the steppes, along with his small band of supporters, seizing and losing

his dream city, Samarkand, fighting the Uzbegs and venturing into Russia and the Gobi desert. Of these trying "throneless times" Babur writes: "It passed through my mind that to wander from mountain to mountain, homeless and houseless, had nothing to recommend it," and goes on to confess that he often felt like crying. But he spent some carefree years at Kabul, where the only sorrow or distress he faced were "on account of the ringlets of some beloved one."

The builders of Samarkand had given Babur his first taste of Hindustan. Legend also has it that in his wanderings in the steppes Babur once met a 111-year old shepherdess. For a whole night this woman narrated tales of Hindustan, whetting Babur's appetite

to see the "land of the Ganges." He made four unsuccessful attempts to invade Hindustan. Finally, in 1526, on the historic field of Panipat, 50 km north of Delhi, Babur defeated and slew Sultan Ibrahim, unpopular ruler of the crumbling Lodi dynasty. Babur was outnumbered ten to one, but he was aided by that rare Chinese invention, gunpowder. Three days after the battle Babur marched into Delhi and proclaimed himself emperor. The *khutba*, the Friday afternoon sermon, was read in his name. The people listened in silence, a fact which was seen as a token of assent.

Babur found nothing attractive about Hindustan, and lists its disadvantages very specifically in his memoirs. He ruled for a mere four years, and at his death on 25 December 1530, Humayun ascended the throne. As a person Humayun was ill-equipped to strengthen the nebulous empire he had inherited. In a few years he was temporarily ousted by an Afghan noble, Sher Shah. Humayun fled to the deserts of Sind, and in Umarkot on 15 October 1542 his wife gave birth to Akbar. Unable to award his followers the gifts customary at the birth of a prince, Humayun handed them musk, saying, "This is all the present I can afford to make you on this birth of my son whose fame will, I trust, be one day expanded all over the world as the perfume of the musk now fills this tent." How true these words were to prove!

Humayun regained his empire for a brief, restful year, and on his death in 1556, Akbar, a mere child of thirteen, ascended the throne. In later years, it was Akbar who was to have the most profound influence on Shah Jahan.

For the first few years of his reign, Akbar was under the guardianship of Bairam Khan. Thereafter he took things into his own hands, proving himself more competent at each step. It was Akbar who undoubtedly consolidated the empire, and it was under him that it became the great Moghul Empire. Akbar told his biographer, Abul Fazl: "A monarch should ever be intent on conquest, otherwise his enemies would rise in arms against him." And he kept his word. By 1601, Kashmir, Sind, Kandahar, Kabul, Gujarat, Berar, Gondwana and other lesser territories were annexed to the empire.

But Akbar's accomplishments did not end with his conquests. If in building the Taj Mahal Shah Jahan had captured the very essence of architecture, surely he learnt much from Akbar himself. For his grandfather built not only the impressive Agra Fort, he

The chief beauty of the Taj mausoleum lies in its luminous and majestic dome, believed to have been built by Ismail Afandi from Turkey. It is in fact a double dome. At its base on the outside are four chattris *or kiosks which provide the balance for its extraordinary height.*

5

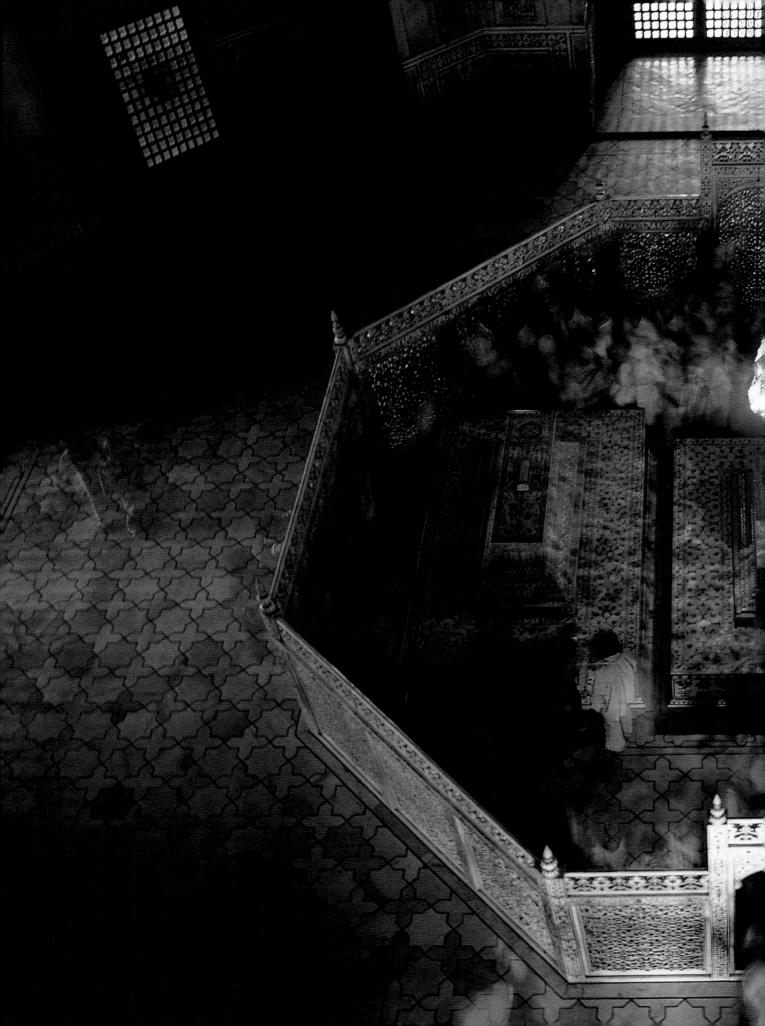

also founded the magnificent city of Fatehpur Sikri. In spite of his harem of over 300 wives, Akbar had no sons. So he sought the blessings of the Sufi saint, Salim Chisthi, who lived in the village of Sikri near Agra. Akbar was told he would have three sons. On 30 August 1569 the first one was born, whom Akbar named Salim—later to be Jahangir—after the saint, though he always called him Shaikhu Baba. True to the prophecy, two more sons were born to Akbar. To commemorate the birth of his sons, Akbar built Fatehpur Sikri. Abul Fazl wrote: "His majesty plans splendid edifices, and dresses the work of his mind and heart in stone and clay." The city was completed in fourteen years, and Akbar not only designed many structures himself, but was often with the masons at the construction site.

At Fatehpur Sikri he built the Ibadat Khana, the House of Worship. Akbar had by now acquired an aura of divinity. His tolerant attitude towards other religions would be sadly forgotten by Jahangir, and towards the close of his reign, even by Shah Jahan. Though illiterate himself, Akbar held learned discourses with theologians from all over the world. To the Ibadat Khana came Hindus, Zoroastrians, Jains, Taoist and Confucian scholars from China, Sufis from Bukhara, Buddhists from Sri Lanka and Christians from Goa. They marvelled at Akbar's curiosity and at his efforts to understand the

Preceding pages 6-7: The Taj Mahal is a glorious culmination of the artistic fusion of Indian architecture and Moghul ornamentation. It was built over a period of twenty-two years (1632-54), with a labour force of approximately 20,000 workers, at a monumental cost that has never been precisely tabulated. The work was supervised by experienced architects like Makramat Khan and Mir Abdul Karim, though there can be no doubt that the ultimate vision and guidance was Shah Jahan's alone.
Pages 8-9: An aerial view of the Taj Mahal, framed between the Jamuna to its north and the charbagh garden to its south. Visible in the background is the sandstone gateway to the Taj.
Pages 10-11: The cenotaphs of Shah Jahan and Mumtaz Mahal surrounded by a marble screen in the large octagonal memorial chamber.

Babur (1483-1530). A Chagatai Turk hailing from Samarkhand, Babur laid the foundations in 1526 of the Moghul dynasty which was to rule Hindustan for 300 years.

Akbar (1542-1605). The grandest Moghul of all, Akbar was an outstanding statesman and an enlightened and secular visionary. His architectural heritage is the Agra Fort and Fatehpur Sikri.

Shah Jahan (1592-1666). The greatest builder of the Moghul dynasty, Shah Jahan's timeless legacy is the Red Fort in Delhi and the Taj Mahal in Agra.

Humayun (1508-1556). Sadly bereft of regal attributes, Humayun was ousted in 1540, to regain the throne of Hindustan in 1555, a year before his death.

Jahangir (1569-1627). Married to the illustrious Nur Jahan, Jahangir was a tolerant and indulgent ruler. His lasting contribution was towards the refinement of the arts.

Aurangzeb (1618-1707). The last of the Grand Moghuls, Aurangzeb was an austere and puritanical ruler, who rigidly enforced the Islamic faith throughout his empire.

essence of each religion. Each group thought that the emperor would accept their religion but they were eventually disappointed on this score.

Along with these learned theologians and philosophers there was the shrewd financier, Raja Todar Mal; the brilliant general, Abdur Rahim Khan-i-Khanan; the poet Faizi; the writer Abul Fazl; the musician Tansen and many more skilled artists. The atmosphere of the court was charged by this unusual concentration of intellectuals, poets and writers.

Akbar had a library of 24,000 volumes—books that were not collected but compiled. In other words, his court had not only the best artists, but the best calligraphers as well. The emperor had inherited two Persian artists from his father. These were assisted by Hindu artists of the Gujarati school. With personal encouragement from Akbar, miniature painting achieved an exquisiteness of detail. But the form was to really flower under the patronage of Jahangir, who had a better developed overall sense of design. Jahangir had inherited the poetic aspect of Akbar's nature, though unfortunately not his more statesmanlike one and the representation of nature in miniature painting reached perfection in Jahangir's time.

Following pages 14-15: The Taj Mahal as seen from the Agra Fort, barely a kilometre away across the river Jamuna.

Pages 16-17: The lower burial chamber with the two gravestones of Mirza Ghiyas Beg (father of Nur Jahan and prime minister to Jahangir) and his wife, Asmat Begum, in Itmad-ud-Daulah's mausoleum in Agra. Asmat Begum's tomb lies at the centre of the chamber, while the nobleman was buried by her side—a pattern that was replicated in the Taj Mahal. The subdued light entering through the latticed screen imparts an appropriate sobriety to the chamber. There is an exceptional display of marble inlay work on the walls in striking geometric and flowing designs.

Pages 18-19: An aerial view of Fatehpur Sikri, Akbar's capital city for fifteen years, built as his grateful offering to the Sufi saint, Sheikh Salim Chisti, who had prophesied the birth of heirs to the emperor. In the spacious courtyard of Fatehpur's Jami Masjid stands the holy marble shrine of the saint.

Emperor Babur and Moghul standards. (*Babur Nama, courtesy, National Museum, New Delhi*).

Akbar also had the Turki chronicles of Timur translated into Persian, and the court elders were asked to write detailed accounts of their experiences with Babur and Humayun. Abul Fazl himself wrote the *Akbar Nama*, the history of Akbar, and the *Ain-i-Akbari* which was a combination of gazetteer, almanac, dictionary of science, book of rules and procedures, and a statistical digest. These were the books that would influence Jahangir and Shah Jahan, for they instilled in them a deep sense of the history of their dynasty.

In 1585, Akbar moved his court to the Punjab. On 5 January 1592, in the magnificent palace at Lahore, Jahangir's Hindu wife bore him a son, later to be named Shah Jahan. Jahangir records the birth in his memoirs: "To Jagat Gosain, daughter of Mota Raja Uday Singh, was born Sultan Khurram in the thirty-sixth year of my father's reign. His advent made the world joyous." Akbar chose the name Khurram, which means joyous, because he said his birth made the world glad. It was also noted that Prince Khurram was born in the first millennium, and like his father, in the same month as the Prophet. Khurram was a well-loved child, doted upon by his father and grandfather. He was put under the charge of Ruqiah Sultan Begum, the honoured wife of Akbar and it is said that she loved him a thousand times more than if he had been her own son. That he was a very special favourite of Akbar's there is no doubt.

When Khurram was four years, four months and four days old he was circumcised, and thereafter began his education, a process of learning that would develop not only his mind but his heart and hands as well. Over the years, the Sufis became Khurram's favourite teachers. Hakim Ali Gilani taught him science and medicine, and later in life, as emperor, Khurram was to remember him as the wisest man he had ever known. From other Sufis he learnt grammar, logic, mathematics, astronomy and geology. He learnt Arabic, the language of the Koran, and Persian, the language of the court. He developed his skill as a rider and swordsman. His teachers said of him that he "possessed a sharp wit, a wonderful memory, a love for detail, and the capacity to master

them." This last quality he certainly inherited from his father, Jahangir.

There was more to Khurram's education. In 1597, Akbar had him put under Mir Murad Juwaini to learn military strategy. Raja Salivahan taught him rifle shooting. And so many discussions did Khurram have with his grandfather and father about architecture that by the time he was fifteen he was already being asked to remodel old palaces and design parts of new ones.

In Jahangir's memoirs, Khurram's growth is lovingly recorded: ". . . and gradually as his years increased so did his excellence. He was more attentive to my father than all my other children . . . there is no comparison between him and the other children." "Truly," wrote Jahangir, "he is my real child."

Khurram is said to have spent as much time as possible with Akbar, who often himself instructed him on matters military and otherwise. And when the great emperor lay dying, Khurram refused to leave his bedside: "So long as there is one breath of life in Shah Baba, nothing can induce me to leave him," he said.

In 1605, when Khurram was thirteen years old, Jahangir became the emperor. Jahangir was the beneficiary of Akbar's wisdom and shrewdness and for fifteen years at least he enjoyed a peaceful reign. If there were rumblings, the cause lay in his persecution of the Jains and Sikhs. His attitude to religion was directed by impulse rather than policy. While he held dialogues with Hindu ascetics and Jesuit priests, he had temples desecrated and Sikh gurus tortured.

And what of the splendours of Jahangir's court? It is known that painting reached its height under his patronage, that artists always accompanied him lest he come upon a bird or flower that he wished to be copied. Edward Terry, an English clergyman who came to India in 1617, writes that Jahangir was "the greatest and richest master of precious stones that inhabits the whole earth." History, however, has proved that Shah Jahan outshone him on this score. Not that Jahangir's penchant for opulence was any the less—wearing a robe studded with jewels, which took six years to embroider, eating from dishes that were moulded from precious metals, carrying jewel-encrusted weapons, satisfying every whim and fancy regardless of the inconvenience others would have to suffer. A classic example of the last is when he sent a courtier all the way to China to replace a cup the man had accidentally broken. The finest of everything—whether carpets, jewels, paintings, animals, embroideries or perfumes—were found in the court. Craftsmen and artisans were patronized in the truest sense of the word; it had been the case in Akbar's time, and it would be so with Shah Jahan too. Moghul artefacts and architecture that have survived

Under the influence of alcohol Jahangir is said to have indulged in great cruelties. Unfortunately, as the years went by he became increasingly addicted to alcohol and opium. There was a third, overpowering factor in Jahangir's life—his queen Nur Jahan. Nur Jahan was of pure Persian blood. Her father, Ghiyas Beg, had been reduced to poverty in his native Khorasan. Helped by a merchant, he and his family made the rough journey to Agra where in no time he proved his worth at Akbar's court. It is said that Jahangir saw Mehr-un-Nisa (as Nur Jahan was earlier known) some time in 1607, and fell in love with her instantly. He did

An aerial view of the entrance of Akbar's tomb at Sikandra, ten km from Agra.

to this day prove that the emperors were more than rewarded for their patronage. As for painters, Jahangir is said to have pampered them like his own children. But if the Moghuls had a love for art and architecture, they also indulged in forms of entertainment and punishment that seem utterly incongruous with their innate sense of refinement. But in those days for the emperor to indulge in bizarre acts was considered as acceptable and natural as the jewelled plume on his turban. Such was the atmosphere Khurram grew up in.

away with all obstructions, including her husband (so the tale goes), that lay in his path. Finally, he won her and in 1611 she became his favourite queen—Nur Jahan, Light of the World.

But meanwhile, what of Khurram in the year 1607? He was a young prince of fifteen, with an excellent intellectual background, a highly developed aesthetic sense, accustomed to the essence of luxury and refinement, his father's favourite, and with his aristocratic nose, high forehead and large languid eyes, well on his way to becoming the most handsome of the Moghuls.

It was to be a momentous year for Khurram. An event took place at the royal Meena Bazaar, which was the private market attached to the harem. Here the women of the aristocracy used to purchase their endless requirements. This was their *sanctum sanctorum.* The Meena Bazaar also served as the royal post exchange. No male dared trespass here, except in those two or three days each month when the place was transformed. The men of the court would flock to it as the women of the harem—wives and concubines—posed as shopkeepers, haggling even with the mightiest. Bearing in mind the inflexible formality of court life, this

protested, or so the legend goes. No, this was no piece of glass but a rare diamond. It cost a vast fortune—ten thousand rupees—a sum even he could not afford, she added boldly. It is said that Khurram took the exact amount out of his sleeve, gave her the money, picked up the piece of glass and left—with the image of Arjumand Banu deeply imprinted in his mind.

The next day Khurram made an unusual and bold request to his father. Unusual and bold because in those days one did not marry for love alone. He sought the hand of Arjumand Banu in marriage. It is said that Jahangir smiled mysteriously—recalling perhaps his own love

Left: *Details from Akbar's tomb at Sikandra.*

Right: *The exquisite workmanship on the interior walls of the tomb at Sikandra, timeless in its magnificence.*

must have been an occasion eagerly awaited by both sexes.

Khurram strolled through the Meena Bazaar, princely, elegant and waited upon by courtiers. His penetrating eyes caught a glimpse of a beautiful girl hawking silk and glass beads. In a trice he was at her stall, and indeed, such beauty he had never seen. She was Arjumand Banu, the highborn and exquisite daughter of Asaf Khan, brother of Nur Jahan. How strange, then, that word of her beauty had not filtered through the harem. He saw a piece of glass at her stall and asked its worth. Arjumand Banu

for Nur Jahan—and silently raised his right hand in assent.

Five years were to pass before Khurram would once again gaze upon the loveliness of Arjumand Banu. In the meanwhile, for political reasons, Khurram was married to Quandari Begum, a princess of the Persian royal family. Monogamy was not suitable for princes and emperors, and Khurram did not forget Arjumand Banu; if anything, his passion for her increased.

In 1607 also, this "lofty son of fortune," as Jahangir refers to Khurram in his memoirs, was awarded the *jagir* of Hissar Firoz and given the right to pitch a red tent—honours traditionally reserved for the crown prince, honours that his three brothers Khusrau, Parwiz and Shahriyar had been denied.

In Khurram's sixteenth year, Jahangir records an event:

> . . . the astrologers and astronomers represented that a most important epoch, according to his horoscope, would occur as the prince's health had not been good and I gave an order that they should weigh him according to the prescribed rules,

auspicious for Khurram to wed Arjumand Banu. He was a regal twenty-year-old; she, an exquisite flower of nineteen. It was a grand wedding, as may well be expected. Jahangir and Khurram went in procession, surrounded by nobles, musicians and dancers, acrobats, rare animals in cages, slaves, dervishes and priests. Indeed, the wealth, the pomp and the splendour were unprecedented.

Jahangir himself adorned Khurram with the wedding wreath of pearls. And on the bride too he bestowed great honours.

Mumtaz Mahal's father was Asaf Khan, brother to Nur Jahan and the prime minister

The tomb of Itmad-ud-Daulah was designed by his daughter, the empress Nur Jahan, and completed in 1628. It is a platform tomb with four short minarets and epitomizes a perfect synthesis of Indian and Islamic architectural elements.

against gold, silver and other metals, which should be divided among the fakirs and needy. The whole of the day was passed in pleasure and many of his presents were approved.

Nothing extraordinary occurred for the next three years. Still, the entry reveals the importance given to astrologers, and tells us about a custom common in those times— weighing a prince or an emperor against jewels and precious metals.

The astrologers chose the year 1612 as

of Shah Jahan. Her grandfather was the respected Itmad-ud-Daulah. Her family, in a way, was almost an extension of the royal family. Even her mother, Diwanji Begum, belonged to the Persian nobility. Mumtaz grew up in her father's harem, indulged by all. She learnt Arabic and Persian, and was deeply influenced by Nur Jahan. Nur Jahan was no ordinary woman. She designed clothes and jewellery, was well read and hunted tigers! Politically, she was shrewd and ambitious. And as Jahangir's addiction to opium and alcohol increased, so did Nur

Jahan's power over him. Soon the emperor was a puppet in her hands. He is known to have said: "All I desire is a cup of wine and a piece of meat; to rule the kingdom I have Nur Jahan." History has proved that it was more a case of misrule.

Fortunately, Mumtaz Mahal was unlike her aunt in this aspect. She was compassionate, generous and demure. And what of her legendary beauty? No actual likeness of her's could exist, because the women were in *purdah*. At most, the painter could look upon a reflection in a mirror. There is one painting by a court artist and it is said to be of Mumtaz

and Mumtaz Mahal other than that it was idyllic. It is said that the two were inseparable, never more than a room away from each other. She even accompanied him when he went to fight wars. Ladies-in-waiting, children, all the paraphernalia of the harem followed the young prince. In her nineteen years of marriage, Mumtaz Mahal bore fourteen children, seven of whom died in infancy.

In 1614, Khurram conducted his first military campaign. Four years earlier he had proved his bravery by striking a tiger with his sword and saving Jahangir's life. Now he marched against the Rana of Mewar and the young prince

Details from the facade of Itmad-ud-Daulah's tomb. The Moghul art of inlay work that covers all its walls was perfected here. Different colours of precious stone inlay have been used to create geometrical designs and floral motifs, with outstanding effect.

Mahal—a woman with aristocratic features, almost perfect in their loveliness; black plaited hair and a jewelled head-dress framing a face that is at once innocent and sensuous. She has been described as having "soft black eyes, delicately pencilled eyebrows, long, silky lashes and velvet skin like lilies." Court poets would celebrate her beauty; the moon, they said, hid its face in shame before Mumtaz Mahal. And she was known not only for her beauty but for her warmth, her candour, and her straightforwardness.

Little is known of the private life of Khurram

proved himself to be a brilliant general and diplomat. Of his celebrated return, Jahangir writes, "I called that son forward and embraced him and having kissed his head and face, favoured him with special kindness and

Following pages 26-27: *In its extensive use of white marble, of screens enclosing the imitation cenotaphs on the top floor and the delicacy of its inlay work the mausoleum of Itmad-ud-Daulah was to an extent a prelude to the Taj. A synthesis of design and colour is the real achievement of this monument.*

greetings . . . gave him a special dress of honour . . . a coat of gold brocade, a rosary of pearls . . . a special horse with a jewelled saddle and a special elephant."

Khurram was to earn more laurels in 1616, with his victories in the Deccan, from where he brought back many precious gifts for Jahangir. He was received with "exceeding kindness and uncontrolled delight." And Khurram, who was considered by Jahangir to be in all respects his first son, was given the title of Shah Sultan Khurram.

It seems that for all his princely ways, Khurram did not drink wine. Jahangir wrote in 1616:

Up to the present year, when he is twenty-four years old and is married and has children, he has never defiled himself with drinking wine. On this day, when the assembly for his weighing was held, I said to him, "Baba! Thou hast become the father of children and kings and kings' sons have drunk wine. Today . . . I will give thee wine to drink, and give thee leave to drink on feast days, at the time of the New Year, and at great festivals. But thou must observe the path of moderation for wise men do not consider it right to drink to such an extent as to destroy the understanding, and it is necessary that from drinking only profit should be derived."

In 1618, Jahangir presented his beloved son with the first copy of his journal, the *Jahangir Nama*. Khurram's life became increasingly political as his father entrusted him with more campaigns. Mumtaz Mahal was ever at his side and proved herself to be an intelligent political advisor. She became Khurram's trusted confidante.

In the next few years, however, the idyllic existence of these young lovers was disrupted by the scheming Nur Jahan. Resenting the increasing importance given to Khurram, she instigated a series of plots that eventually led the young prince to rebel openly. Jahangir was completely in the hands of Nur Jahan. No longer was Khurram his "son of lofty fortune"; instead Jahangir refers to him as *Bi-daulat*, the Wretch. Khurram's sons, Dara Shikoh and Aurangzeb were hostages at the royal court. But Nur Jahan's schemes were finally foiled by Khurram and Asaf Khan joining forces. Khurram's brothers, Parwiz Khusrau and Shahriyar, had been dispensed with along with other rivals. They were the losers in a bloody war of succession, in which Khurram emerged triumphant. In the words of a contemporary writer, it was "entirely lawful for the great sovereigns to rid this mortal world of the existence of their brothers and other relations, whose very annihilation is conducive to common good." And when Jahangir died, sick and broken on 29 October 1627, Khurram was declared emperor.

The grand coronation was held at Agra on 4 February 1628. Shah Sultan Khurram became Shah

Mumtaz Mahal (1593-1631), was the favourite wife of Emperor Shah Jahan. Born Arjumand Banu, she first met Shah Jahan when she was just fourteen years old in a monthly bazaar held in the palace premises. It was love at first sight for both and Shah Jahan promptly secured his father's assurance for her hand in marriage. After marriage she became Shah Jahan's constant, loyal and faithful companion, bearing him fourteen children, of which only seven survived. She died prematurely and tragically in the nineteenth year of their marriage, during childbirth.

Jahan, Emperor of the World. He inherited an enormous empire. For those who had helped him there were exotic gifts; for rivals there was only the sword. And his beloved queen was showered with even more splendour. Shah Jahan built magnificent apartments for her at the Agra Fort. They were described in the *Shah Jahan Nama* as "the Paradise-like buildings of Her Exalted Chaste Majesty, the Queen of the World, the Begum Sahiba." Known as the Khas Mahal, they were the most sumptuous of all palaces of the time. From these rooms in white marble, Mumtaz Mahal must have gazed at the very spot where now stands her mausoleum.

Shah Jahan's trust and confidence in her judgement increased; eventually he gave her the royal seal, Muhr Uzah. Not even the emperor could change his mind once the seal had been put. Mumtaz Mahal continually interceded on behalf of petitioners and gave allowances to widows and orphans. She was, in short, a model of feminine virtue. But even she, it is said, enjoyed the spectacle of animals and men fighting; it is also said that Shah Jahan persecuted the Portuguese at Hoogly at her instigation.

Shah Jahan also lived in palaces ornamented with ruby-encrusted arabesques and ceilings of gold, palaces that were strewn with the most exquisitely embroidered tapestries, the most finely woven carpets, with enamelled lamps using scented oil, gold decanters and boxes of pearls and silver candlesticks, to mention just a few of the fineries; palaces through which flowed scented fountains. Such opulence did not, however, mean that the emperor luxuriated in his harem all day. In fact, he had a rather tiring schedule. His day began at 4.00 a.m. Thereafter followed prayers, audiences to the public, court sessions at the Diwan-i-Am and Diwani-i-Khas (the halls of public and private audiences respectively), and at the very exclusive Shah Burj, or Royal Tower. There was an elaborate midday meal at the harem, followed by a brief siesta. And then the emperor attended to problems within the harem. More prayers, more administrative matters, supper and entertainment at the harem and then to bed by ten. But there was always time for Mumtaz Mahal. She was never far from his thoughts, and whenever possible, at his side.

Shah Jahan (1592-1666), the Grand Moghul, met Arjumand Banu when he was fifteen, married her when he was twenty and remained in love with her till their last days together. He rewarded her exceptional loyalty by giving her the title of Mumtaz Mahal, or Chosen One of the Palace and the sole authority to use the Royal Seal. She encouraged him in his passion for architecture. Though she only survived long enough after his coronation to see the ongoing reconstruction in marble of the Khas Mahal in the Agra Fort, her demise spurred him to construct in her memory the magnificient Taj Mahal, one of the seven wonders of the world.

In 1630, when Shah Jahan set out for Burhanpur to subdue the forces of Khan Jahan Lodi, she accompanied him, even though she was expecting her fourteenth child. Shah Jahan was reluctant to let her undergo the long journey to the heart of the Deccan; but the queen was adamant, and finally, she had her way.

They reached Burhanpur, and on 7 June 1631 the child was born even as the battle was on. News of the birth was sent to Shah Jahan as he surveyed the scene of battle. A healthy baby girl, he

was told; but there was no news of Mumtaz Mahal. However, he waited patiently. Finally, he received a message to say that the queen was well, but wanted to be left alone to rest. Relieved at the news, Shah Jahan himself soon retired for the night. But at dawn he was summoned by his favourite daughter, Jahanara. The queen had taken a turn for the worse. The emperor rushed across to Mumtaz Mahal's tent, and everyone except Wazir Khan, her doctor, and Sati-un-Nissa, her favourite lady-in-waiting, were asked to leave. The doctor feared ill, for Mumtaz had told him that she had heard her child crying in her womb. That was a bad omen. The queen was dying.

It is said that as Shah Jahan knelt by his beloved queen, she whispered to him to build for her a monument that would symbolize the purity and beauty of their love. A short while later she died. And Shah Jahan, the great Emperor of the World, the grandest of the Moghuls, broke down and wept inconsolably.

An aerial view of Agra Fort. A historical legacy that has survived the ravages of time for 450 years. Built by Akbar, the third Moghul emperor, and added to by his son Jahangir and grandson Shah Jahan, the fort is built in a bow-like form with its straight side running **along the river. It lies two kilometres** *west of th Taj Mahal. Jahangir and Shah Jahan added palaces, audience halls and a mosque in the fort. While Akbar drew on Islamic and Hindu traditions, by Shah Jahan's time the style had become so homogenized that it was impossible to separate the Hindu and Muslim strands.*

A Dream Fulfilled

For a week Shah Jahan remained behind closed doors. He neither ate nor drank; nor did he allow anyone in. Those who sat by his door said they heard a low, continuous moan. He emerged on the eighth day, an old man. His hair had turned white, his back was bent, his face worn with despair.

Shah Jahan's life would never be the same again. Mumtaz Mahal had been too precious a part of it. For nineteen years she had been his constant companion; more recently, first lady of the court and keeper of the royal seal. She had been his trusted advisor, mother of his children and above all, his own beloved. No traditional forty-day mourning period would suffice for her. The entire kingdom was ordered into mourning for two years and a silent gloom spread over north India. There was no public entertainment or amusement and no music; no jewellery, perfumes and other such fineries were used. Brightly coloured clothes were forbidden. And anyone who dared disrespect the memory of the queen was executed. Shah Jahan himself kept away from the public eye as much as possible. The same emperor who once wore a robe so heavily encrusted with gems that he needed the support of two slaves, was now wearing simple white clothes for much longer than the stipulated period; he who had inherited an enormous empire, spoke of wanting to become a homeless fakir had not the responsibilities of kingship hindered him. So stricken was he that death was not far for him either, or so a court historian records.

Deep in his despair, Shah Jahan had made a decision which in the next few years would become an obsession with him; he would build for his queen a mausoleum more chaste and beautiful than anything that had ever been built. Only that would be good enough for Mumtaz Mahal.

Six months after Mumtaz Mahal's death, her body was brought to Agra. Her second son, Shah Shuja, her favourite lady-in-waiting, Sati-un-Nissa, and the doctor, Wazir Khan, accompanied the body. Shah Jahan ordered mounds of silver to be distributed en route. A piece of land had already been selected for Mumtaz Mahal's burial in Agra, where the queen's body was temporarily buried in a crypt in a silent garden along the banks of the river Jamuna, not even a league away from the Agra Fort. The garden had been purchased from Raja Jaisingh of Amber in exchange for a palace. For the next twenty-two years this silent garden was to be the centre of immense and extraordinary creativity.

In 1631 itself, Shah Jahan had begun to invite designs from architects from south India, Egypt, Burma, Transcaucasia, Persia and Sri Lanka. But the great Moghul was not easy to please, and all the proposals were rejected.

If any one design was accepted, its author remains a mystery. More than three hundred years have passed since the Taj Mahal was completed, but its architect is still unknown. Over the centuries there have been many speculations as to who the architect might have been. Some theories seem probable, others entirely baseless.

At one time it was believed, more so by the Europeans, that the architect of the Taj Mahal had been a Venetian, Geronimo Veroneo. To prove their theory, the Europeans cited Father Sebastian Manrique. Manrique was an Augustinian monk who had travelled to the East in 1628, and settled in the Portuguese colony of Goa. In 1642 another monk, Father Antony, was taken hostage by the Moghuls so Manrique had to travel to Agra to secure his release. He spent twenty-six days in Agra, during which time he visited all the local sights.

Facing page: *The Taj, as seen through the morning mist. 'The Taj is a poem. It is not only a pure architectural type, but also a creation which satisfies the imagination, because its characteristic is Beauty.'*

One of these was a tomb being constructed on the banks of the Jamuna. Apparently, he was deeply impressed by the structure, so much so that he wanted to know who its architect was. Later he was to record his findings in which he wrongly attributed the work of designing the Taj to Veroneo:

> The architect of these works was a Venetian, by name Geronimo Veroneo, who had come to this part in a Portuguese ship, and died in the city of Lahore before he reached it. Fame, the swift conveyor of good and evil news, had spread the story that the Emperor summoned him and informed him that he desired to erect a great and sumptuous tomb for his dead wife, and was required to erect a design for this, for the Emperor's inspection. The architect Veroneo carried out this order and within a few days proved the great skill he had in his way of procuring several models of the most beautiful architecture. He pleased the ruler in respect of his designs, but in his barbarous pride and arrogance, His Majesty was displeased with him owing to his low estimate, and it is said that becoming very angry, he told Veroneo to spend three crores of rupees . . . and to inform him when it was expended.

It is true that Veroneo did come to India. He lived and prospered for a while in Agra. In fact he lies buried in the Christian Cemetery of Padre Santos in Agra. However, contemporary and later records do not support Manrique's theory. Veroneo's European friends in Agra referred to him as a jeweller. Peter Mundy, a seventeenth century English traveller, knew Veroneo personally and visited him while the Taj Mahal was under construction. Had Veroneo indeed been the architect, Mundy, a careful observer, would have definitely made note of the fact. Tavernier also does not speak of Veroneo as the designer. Persian sources make no mention of him either. In English factory records he is alluded to as an Italian jeweller, and Father Francis Corsi, intimately connected with the Europeans at Agra and Lahore, says that Veroneo had "fine hands and a great skill for making curious pieces in gold set with precious stones."

In 1844, Major Sleeman, well known for documenting his travels in the state of Oudh, proposed another European candidate as the possible architect of the Taj Mahal. Sleeman wrote: ". . . the magnificent building (the Taj Mahal) and all the palaces of Agra and Delhi were, I believe, designed by Austin de Bordeaux, a Frenchman of great talent and merit, in whose ability and integrity the Emperor placed much reliance."

Austin de Bordeaux was a silversmith, who, it is said, dealt in counterfeit gems in France. He came to India in the early seventeenth century and found work with Jahangir; he stayed on as a throne-maker to Shah Jahan. It is possible that Veroneo and Austin de Bordeaux contributed to the gold work on the thrones and ceilings of the royal palaces. Bordeaux died in 1632; and in a letter now preserved in the Bibliotheque Nationale in Paris, he reveals a lack of interest in architecture. Veroneo and Bordeaux lose out on another count too: it was well known that Mumtaz Mahal was unsympathetic to Christians. It is unlikely, then, that Shah Jahan would have asked a Christian to design her mausoleum.

Such tangible proofs apart, the Taj Mahal speaks for itself. There is very obviously nothing European about it. Ustad Ahmad, a Persian engineer, mathematician, architect and astrologer, was known to frequently direct the emperor's architectural projects. He is also said to have designed the Taj Mahal. But this theory too has a catch. This fact has been mentioned by his son; and it is well known that sons often eulogize their fathers to add a touch of grandeur to their ancestry.

In all probability, if any one person made a major contribution to the design of the Taj Mahal it was a Turk named Ustad Isa Afandi. Several sources mention his name. It is believed that his design embodied much of what the emperor wanted to express. So Shah Jahan ordered a wooden model to be made of his design. After modifications, he gave his final approval.

Fortunately, we know somewhat more about the artisans who worked on the Taj Mahal. The lavish patronage accorded by Akbar and Jahangir had lured many of the artisans back from Samarkand, descendants of those whom Timur had taken with him. In Shah Jahan's time the patronage was, if anything, more extensive; and the finest engineers, carvers and stonemasons of the East were to be found in his ateliers. The names of the chief artisans who worked on the Taj Mahal have been recorded. Ismail Afandi, who designed hemispheres and built domes, was amongst the foremost. He came from Turkey, where he had worked for the great Ottomans. To cast the gold finial that would crown the dome came Qazim Khan from Lahore. He was a renowned worker of precious metals. Chiranji Lal was called from Delhi to pattern the mosaic, for mosaic was fundamental in mosque and tomb designs. From Shiraz in Persia came Amanat Khan, master calligrapher who was ranked as high as the architect.

It is interesting that Amanat Khan's was the only signature thought worthy to be on the walls of the Taj Mahal. At the base of the interior dome, near the lines from the Koran is the inscription: "Written by the insignificant being, Amanat Khan Shirazi." Amanat Khan was assisted by two other calligraphers—Mohammad Khan from Baghdad and Roshan Khan from Syria. The stone cutter (Amir Ali), came from Baluchistan, the mason from Balkh, the engineer from Samarkand, the sculptors from Bukhara and the inlay artisans from south India. It is believed that thirty-seven people comprised the creative nucleus of what was to be the world's most magnificent mausoleum.

If Ustad Isa Afandi contributed to the design, surely Shah Jahan must have done so too? During his travels in the Deccan he must have been inspired by the architecture of the magnificent forts and palaces that he saw, as he had been in his younger days by Akbar's buildings. And what of the Moghul tradition? Modern day architects have pointed out that the Taj Mahal is not an "isolated construction," or a "meteoric idea." It may be matchless in its beauty, but it was part of the natural evolution of a style, marking the perfect stage in the evolution of the tomb. Its precursors in India were the tombs of Emperor Humayun and the Moghul noble, Abdur Rahim Khan-i-Khanan,

both in Delhi, and built within fifty years of each other. For E. B. Havell the Taj is "of a living organic growth, born of the Indian artists' consciousness . . . . The Taj is not an isolated phenomenon, the creation of a single mastermind, but the glorious consummation of a great epoch of art."

It is obvious that great thought and planning must have gone into the making of the Taj Mahal. It is of a perfection that makes itself felt even to the untrained eye. It is not only the mausoleum but the entire setting—the location, the garden, the gateway, the adjacent mosque and Mehman Khana, and the auxiliary buildings—that is perfect.

Only Shah Jahan could afford the grandeur of this scheme. He had ruled from the famed Peacock Throne, with its twelve emerald-studded pillars, each topped by capitals of two jewelled peacocks on either side of a diamond-leafed tree and supporting a canopy of pearls, emeralds, sapphires and gold. And all this indulgence flowed from a treasury said to contain no less than:

> . . . 750 pounds of pearls, 275 pounds of emeralds, 5,000 gems from Cathay, corals, topaz and other less precious stones in almost infinite number, 200 daggers, 1,000 gold studded saddles with jewels, 2 golden thrones, 3 silver thrones, 100 silver chairs, 5 golden chairs, 200 most precious mirrors, 100,000 precious silver plates and utensils, 50,000 pounds of gold plate, wrought gold and silver, Chinese vessels, worked necklaces, cups, discs, candelabras, tubs of uncut diamonds, gold images of elephants, golden bridles, porcelain vessels . . .

This was the treasury at Agra. At Lahore, it was three times this quantity. Manrique, who claims to have been smuggled into Shah Jahan's harem and seen him at supper, says, ". . . he paid scant attention to the dancing . . . spending all the time gazing at these jewels (that had just been gifted to him) and letting them pass through his hands." When Shah Jahan died, Aurangzeb asked for an estimate of his jewels. He was told that it would take an expert fourteen years to assess Shah Jahan's collection!

The marble walls of the Taj Mahal are resplendent with what are popularly known as the 'jewels of the Taj'. Shah Jahan chose the finest material for the embellishment of the monument. White marble was brought from Makrana in Rajasthan, precious stones, like crystal, came from China, lapis lazuli from Sri Lanka, cornelian from Baghdad, turquoise from Tibet, agate from Yemen, coral from the Red Sea, onyx from Persia and chrysolite from Europe. The marble screen enclosing the cenotaphs features an astonishing range of inlay work, some of it inset in single blocks of marble. Some flowers are said to have been recreated with as many as sixty pieces of different precious stones. The delicate floral motif is used repeatedly—reflecting the Moghul love for gardens and flowers. Inlay work in contrasting black marble has also been used for calligraphic inscriptions of scriptural verse, each letter of the inscriptions in the panel cut and set with such precision that a needle point passed over the stone is said to meet with no obstruction.

Details from the central arch of the gateway to the Taj.

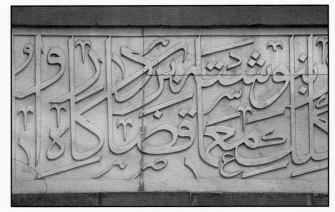

Calligraphic inscriptions inlaid on white marble.

The side arches of the Taj are perfect replicas of the main entrance arch.

One of the two buildings flanking the Taj.

Stucco inlay on red sandstone in the mosque.

Mumtaz Mahal's tomb in the upper hall.

The 99 names of Allah on Mumtaz Mahal's tomb.

Cenotaph of Shah Jahan, with profuse inlay work.

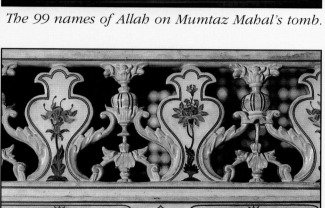

Detail of inlay work on the marble screen.

Detail from a carved marble panel.

Circular inlay motif on Shah Jahan's cenotaph.

Close-up of inlay work on marble.

Intricate work on the base of onion-shaped dome.

Inkwell over Shah Jahan's cenotaph.

Still, to adorn the Taj Mahal, jewels came from every corner of the world; turquoise from Tibet, lapis lazuli from Afghanistan, jasper from Cambay, jade and crystal from China, rare shells, corals and mother-of-pearl from the Indian Ocean, cornelian from Baghdad, chrysolite from Egypt, diamonds from Golconda, quartz from the Himalayas. In addition there was agate, chalcedony, sardonyx, amethyst and black marble. In all, forty-three varieties of precious and semi-precious stones. The exquisite white marble came from the quarries of Makrana in Rajasthan, the red sandstone from Fatehpur Sikri and

Tasimacan, "a great bazaar or marketplace, composed of six courts all encompassed with porticoes under which there were warehouses for merchants." But Tasimacan grew by the day; soon it was on the important caravan route, and not much later, busier than Agra itself. By this time it had been renamed Mumtazabad after the dead queen. Shah Jahan went there regularly to note the progress of the work. And work had begun in earnest. Tavernier notes: "I witnessed the commencement and accomplishment of this great work, on which they have expended years, during which 20,000 men worked incessantly; this is sufficient to

Aerial view of the Taj. On the opposite bank of the river are the ruins of an old foundation where Shah Jahan had intended to build a mausoleum for himself in black marble replicating the Taj. But Aurangzeb, his parsimonious son, thwarted the plan.

Bharatpur. Both are said to have been gifted to the emperor by vassal states. From the imperial treasury came 40,000 tolas (466.55 kg) of gold valued then at six hundred thousand rupees.

When Mumtaz Mahal's body reached Agra it was temporarily buried in a crypt in the garden of the estate acquired for building her tomb. Very soon after this, in 1632, work began on the Taj Mahal. For twenty-two years, 20,000 people laboured to construct the Taj. The silent area beyond the present-day car park and shopping arcade was once a teeming city where the labourers lived. It was first known as

enable one to realize that the cost of it had been enormous . . ."

Today, the mausoleum and its environs are silent; indeed the Taj seems to *create* a silence. But in the twenty-two years during its construction, the scene must have been so very different.

The river Jamuna had been diverted to the foot of the foundations, so that the vista from the completed tomb would be improved. An excavated area, larger than three football fields, was filled with sediment to avoid seepage; and an enormous brick scaffolding was set up. It is not known why the traditional wooden scaffolding was not used. The story goes that once the Taj Mahal was ready, Shah Jahan was told that the scaffolding would take five years to remove. Apparently he gave an order that the people could keep the bricks they removed; the scaffolding is said to have come down overnight!

A ten mile long ramp of tamped earth had been laid through Agra for the transportation of material. On this traversed an unending parade of elephants and bullock-carts dragging blocks of marble to the building site. Manrique again gives an eyewitness account:

> Blocks of white marble had been brought there from over 40 leagues away for the erection of these edifices. Some of these blocks, which I met on the way . . . were of such unusual size and length that they drew the sweat of many powerful teams of oxen and of fierce-looking, big-horned buffaloes, which were dragging enormous, strongly-made wagons, in teams of twenty or thirty animals.

Once the marble reached the site, it was hoisted into place in the same manner as the stone slabs must have been for the Pyramids— by a complicated post and beam pulley, manned by teams of mules and thousands of workers. Peter Mundy gives an idea of the speed of construction. In 1632 itself he writes: "There is already about her tomb a rail of gold. The building is begun and goes on with excessive labour and cost, prosecuted with extraordinary diligence, gold and silver esteemed common metal, and marble but as ordinary stones." This gold rail studded with gems and valued at Rs 600,000 was removed in 1642 for fear of vandals, even though, as Tavernier says, ". . . a eunuch in command of 2,000 men guards both the tomb of the Begum and the Tasimacan."

Even while the construction was underway, a memorial service was held on the death anniversary of the queen. Each year the service became more elaborate. According to an inscription above the gateway of the Taj Mahal, the tomb was completed in 1642. The entire complex, however, was to take another twelve years; Tavernier notes that work was over by 1654. And the memorial service that year was no ordinary one. Solid silver doors graced the entrance to the tomb, and a sheet of pearls was spread over the cenotaph. Silver candle sticks and gold lamps were attached to the walls and the finest Persian carpets covered the floors. The emperor had invited the highest nobles of the land to attend the service.

Tavernier records that Shah Jahan wanted to build his own mausoleum as a replica of the Taj Mahal, but Aurangzeb disapproved of this plan and forced Shah Jahan to change his

The image of the Taj mirrored in the slow waters of the Jamuna to the north.

mind. In 1658 Aurangzeb deposed Shah Jahan and imprisoned him at the Agra Fort where Shah Jahan's life turned more austere by the day. He died on 22 January 1666, after a brief illness. In deference to his wishes, his body was taken down next morning by boat to the Taj Mahal, and he was buried next to his beloved Mumtaz Mahal.

A Flawless Oriental Pearl

Even the casual visitor will notice that every aspect of the Taj Mahal is perfectly proportionate and symmetrical. It is ironical that the one asymmetrical feature is the cenotaph of the man who conceived the very idea of this mausoleum. In the Taj Mahal, the garden tomb has reached perfection. In Persia gardens had been created where, "like the tapestry of the kings of Ormuz, the air is perfumed with musk, and the waters of the brooks are the essence of roses." The Moghuls used such gardens as the setting for tombs, and that of the Emperor Humayun in Delhi is among the earliest examples. Fifty years later, not far from it and in the same style, the tomb of Khani-i-Khanan Abdur Rahim was built. Here, there was further experimentation and some change of form. In the Taj Mahal, every defect was removed.

In the entire architectural scheme of the Taj Mahal, the actual tomb occupies a relatively small portion. The complex is planned in the form of a rectangle, aligned north-south, and measuring 579.12 m by 304.8 m. In the centre is a square garden, 304.8 m on each side, which leaves an oblong space at either end of the rectangle. In the south this is taken up by the gateway and the auxiliary buildings; in the north, along the silent riverfront, by the tomb itself.

When Shah Jahan used to visit the Taj Mahal, he would come down the Jamuna on the royal barge from his palace at the Agra fort. Today, a visitor to the Taj has to wind his way through the noisy unattractive city of Agra. But about 0.8 km before the mausoleum, the road turns into a tree-lined avenue as it cuts through a green and silent park, before reaching the small gate at the exterior of the Taj Mahal complex.

Facing page: The Taj Mahal on a clear morning. The pristine purity of the white marble, said to have come from Makrana in Rajasthan, makes the Taj the most enduringly beautiful monument in the world.

Just before this gate, on either side of the road are two octagonal buildings. The one on the left is believed to be the tomb of the Serving Ladies; on the right is the Fatehpuri Mosque, also known as the Stonecutter's Mosque. It earned this name under the British, when it had been taken over by lapidaries who worked and peddled their wares on its steps. However, its religious function has once again been restored. Inside the small gateway that leads into the complex is a shopping arcade. Here too, as in the central courtyard and beyond, were the lively bazaars of Mumtazabad, where goods were brought by caravans from all parts of the world. This narrow arcade opens on to an expansive central courtyard, the Jilo Khana, now used as a car park. At the east end of this courtyard is the tomb of Mumtaz Mahal's faithful lady-in-waiting, Sati-un-Nissa; at another end is the tomb of a royal wife, Sirhinde Begum.

From the centre of the northern wall springs the immense gateway, 45.7 m wide and about 30.5 m high, that leads to the mausoleum. And through its vaulted entrance the visitor will get his first view of the Taj Mahal—distant, ethereal, yet perfectly contained in the archway.

It is worth pausing for a while to admire the gateway and the garden, for soon the Taj Mahal will absorb the visitor's attention completely. The detached gateway is very typical of Islamic architecture. It is meant to serve as a sentinel, necessary to guard the jewels that often lay within. The gateway creates a sense of awe. Symbolically, too, it has meaning, for a gate is a transition point between the inner and the outer worlds and forms an important part of the whole complex.

This three-storeyed gateway, in red sandstone with white marble inlay, rises to a height of 30.5 m. A colossal archway, with arabesque inlay on its spandrels and framed by Koranic inscriptions dominates the facade. Above this rise eleven marble kiosks with

matching open archways, flanked by pilasters. They rise well above the broad octagonal towers at the corners of the structure. These towers are also topped by marble kiosks. Within the gateway, on either side of the central passage are numerous rooms and halls. It seems as if they were designed to confuse and remained unused for over 300 years. They now house offices of the Archaeological Survey of India. The facade is repeated on the northern side of the gateway, which, when viewed from the actual tomb, is in itself an impressive work of architecture. This is the only gateway to the Taj Mahal. Unlike the

western walls. Instead, water pavilions have been built off the boundary walls as part of the garden plan. It is believed that these pavilions once housed the Naqqar Khana, from where music was played.

The sandstone used is a rich, earthy red and in comparison the lush green of the lawns is outstanding. The Moghuls did not construct an edifice in stern isolation, but presented it through auxiliary buildings, gardens and water channels. The garden of the Taj Mahal is in the classic *charbagh* plan, that is, it is divided into four equal parts. In the earlier tombs, the main structure occupied the centre of the garden;

The main gateway to the Taj, viewed from the side. An impressive structure in its own right, the gateway is made of red sandstone, elaborately carved and inscribed with verses from the Koran, and topped with cupolas.

tombs of Humayun and Itmad-ud-Daulah, there are no false gateways on the eastern and

Preceding pages 42-43: *Like most Moghul mausoleums, the Taj Mahal is a garden tomb. The site selected for the mausoleum was the garden of Raja Jai Singh of Jaipur. The spacious garden is laid out in the charbagh style (rectangle divided into four equal parts), with a spacious marble platform at the centre. A row of fountains placed some feet from each other is carried from end to end with a beautiful walkway on both sides. The Taj is situated at the end of the spacious charbagh.*

here the entire expanse of green lies between the gateway and the tomb.

Once this garden nurtured the rarest of fruit trees and the most exotic birds. The latter are no longer there, but it still does have fine trees, well spaced out on the cool lawns. The garden is divided into four equal parts by an intersecting water channel. In the centre is a raised rectangular marble pond which has five lotus-bud fountains. Around the pond are another twenty-four fountains, and twenty-four more each along the centre of the northern and southern channels. All the fountains, therefore, are on the central north-south axis; there are none in the east-west channel to disturb this effect. The channels themselves, bordered by paved footpaths and cypress trees, are not narrow like those at Sikandra; instead they are broad, glistening sheets of water that perfectly mirror the mausoleum.

Water for these channels was drawn by an ingenious method from the neighbouring Bagh Khan-i-Alam. It was supplied through underground pipes, so designed that there was a uniform undiminished pressure on the fountains, irrespective of their distance from the source.

The Persian concept of an ideal, paradise-

entire width of the plot is the first plinth of red sandstone. This plinth has been paved with geometric mosaic, to be repeated only in the flooring of the central hall of the tomb. At either end of the plinth, and flanking the Taj, are two identical buildings in sandstone with marble domes. These three-domed buildings are much more reminiscent of Humayun's Tomb in their ratio of breadth to height and in the marble inlay work. The building on the west of the mausoleum is a mosque; the one on the east is called the *jawab*, or answer. Identical to the mosque, its only purpose seems to be to provide architectural balance. It is

Parallel pavements of red sandstone leading to the main gateway to the Taj. In the centre runs a water channel featuring fountains flanked by rows of trees.

like garden is perfectly embodied in the Taj Mahal. It was Babur who introduced the Persian garden to Hindustan, and the now unkempt Aram Bagh garden in Agra was the first of the many Persian gardens he created. Babur wrote in his memoirs: "In that charmless and disorderly Hind, plots of gardens were soon laid out with order and symmetry, with suitable borders and parterres in every corner, and in every border, rose and narcissus in perfect arrangement."

At the northern end of the Taj Mahal complex, along the riverfront, covering the

believed to have been used as a caravan-serai, for which reason it is also known as the Mehman Khana. As in the actual tomb and the gateway, the facades of both these structures are dominated by an immense archway, the spandrels ornamented with arabesque inlay. The ceilings have been exquisitely painted in floral patterns. The artists have used traditional Indian folk art pigments—*safeda* or white lead, and *hirmichi* or red earth. A thin layer of red earth was laid over the white surface. Thereafter, the design was drawn and the colour scraped off, exposing the white outlines

of the pattern. It was an effective method, using the minimum number of colours, while simultaneously producing tones of light and shade.

These buildings in themselves are beautiful; so is the gateway and the garden. Yet each component has been planned in proportion to the central structure so that while retaining a special perspective of its own, each is subservient to the mausoleum.

Thus the gateway and the garden, the mosque and the Mehman Khana—in their architectural forms and in tones of green, red, white and the shimmering transparency of

changes, so does the colour of the marble, "from the soft dreaminess at dawn and the dazzling whiteness at midday to its cold splendour in the moonlight, when the dome, thin of substances as the air, hangs among the stars like a great pearl. Yet none of these effects can equal those fleeting moments when, softly illuminated by the brief Indian afterglow, it assumes the enchanting tint of a pale and lovely rose."

If the spirit of Mumtaz Mahal is embodied in the mausoleum, it lies in its utterly feminine quality. It is pure and chaste in its subtle milky whiteness, rising effortlessly and majestically

The mosque flanking the Taj Mahal on the left is a smaller version of the Agra Jami Masjid, with three bays and the characteristic triple domes. The distinctive feature of the mosque is the restrained geometrical designs on the walls and on the dome's ceiling, and the use of sandstone.

water—define the space from which rises the Taj Mahal "like a beautiful princess, surrounded by four ladies-in-waiting." The effect is pyramidal, with the expansive lawns, the receding plinths, the minarets, the square tomb and the bulbous dome, topped with the finial.

Is it the quality of the Makrana marble that makes the Taj Mahal so rare? As the light

Facing page: *Corridor of the Taj mosque engraved with a network of designs in white stucco against a background of red sandstone.*

into the sky. It is sensuous in its full, soft contours and delicate ornamentation. And if the tomb embodies the spirit of Mumtaz Mahal, it also reflects the spirit of the times. The Moghul Empire itself was then enjoying the mellow sensuousness that comes with extraordinary wealth and political security.

From the gateway, the Taj Mahal shimmers like a distant jewel, overpowering in its beauty but not in its size. But as one comes closer, something happens; the mausoleum looms larger and larger. It is still feminine, it is still delicate, but now it towers over one to the exclusion of everything else. And one realizes that a master mind must have worked out the proportions of this building. The tomb has a square plan, with chamfered angles, and lies at the centre of the 5.79 m high marble plinth, which in turn lies recessed at the centre of the red sandstone plinth. From the marble plinth is afforded a spectacular view of the river, the distant Agra Fort and the barren landscape of the opposite bank. Drawings of the memoirs of seventeenth and eighteenth century travellers show that earlier the opposite bank too was dotted with houses of nobles and verdant gardens. The perfect proportions are also

The four facades of the tomb are dominated by an immense arch that occupies practically the whole height up to the parapet. As with the gateway, the mosque and the Mehman Khana, the spandrels are ornamented with inlaid arabesque; the arches are framed with Koranic inscriptions in black marble in the Arabic script.

Calligraphic inscriptions were always used in Islamic architecture. The inscriptions served a double purpose; they were an elegant means of ornamentation, and more important, served to display scriptural verses. In the Taj Mahal, the skill of the calligrapher has created an illusion. The script appears to be of the same size from

The intricate motifs on the walkway around the base of the Taj echo the patterns used on the walls and the dome.

defined by the distribution of lines—horizontal and vertical, straight and curved—and by the distribution of solids and voids. Vast expanses of pure marble have been balanced by alcoves that give depth, as well as add to the play of light and shade. The total height of the tomb up to the apex of the finial is 74.22 m. It exceeds the 56.69 m side square by more than 17.07 m. Humayun's tomb is too broad in relation to its height, and so it has a rather heavy, imposing quality. In Khan-i-Khanan's tomb there is a slight improvement. In the Taj Mahal, the proportions have excelled.

the base to the height above the arch. In fact it is not; the size of the letters has been suitably increased in proportion to the height to convey this impression.

The main arch is flanked by smaller double arches, one over the other. The arched alcoves at the chamfered angles of the tomb are of the same size too, but with a slight difference. These alcoves are semi-octagonal in shape, while the ones on the facade are rectangular. And because of their semi-octagonal shape they are visible from any angle, which would not have been possible had they also been rectangular. Each section of the facade is marked by slender pilasters that rise from the level of the plinth to higher than the frieze and are crowned by beautiful pinnacles with lotus bud finials. Four *chattris* (kiosks) flank the dome at the four corners of the tomb, and are a distinctly Hindu feature. They are detached from the dome, and only appear to be part of the drum that forms the base of the dome. Their main purpose is to balance the extraordinary height of the dome.

The dome itself is indeed the crowning glory of the Taj Mahal. From the base to the apex of the finial, it rises to a height of 44.40 m. It is at

central hall itself. The dome rests on a very high drum, which is ornamented so as to accentuate its whiteness. From here the marble blooms into a gentle fullness till it tapers to form the foliated base of the finial, which pierces the skyline.

And what of the four minarets? At Sher Shah's tomb at Sasaram, at the Charburj in Agra, and in the tombs of Akbar and Itmad-ud-Daulah, towers and minarets of varying sizes have been used. But not with the same touch of genius as at the Taj Mahal. Here, they are detached from the central structure, and rise from the four corners of the plinth to a height

View of a part of the entrance parapet at the Taj. The entire facade is decorated with beautiful inlaid work.

once majestic and slender; it towers above the edifice, yet it brings to mind "the softness of a human breast full of milk." There is a restful purity in its outline; it is almost shadowy in its subtle colouring, yet it clearly defines itself against the vast expanse of the sky.

It is a double dome, for which reason the architect was able to raise it to such a height without causing the interior to be disproportionately high. The first surface roofs the hall below, while the second outlines the monument in space. In between the two surfaces is an area almost equal in size to the

Following pages 50-51: Architects have repeatedly used the arch within a rectangle to give the monument its symmetry. Each of the four facades has a huge central arch, flanked by a set of smaller arches on either side.

Pages 52-53: To many, the grandeur of the Taj is complemented by the slender minarets on octagonal bases at the four corners of the marble plinth, detached from the central structure. Built of white marble, each minaret is 133 feet in height, of the most perfect proportions, and surmounted by a splendid cupola supported on eight elegant pillars, reached by a spiral staircase now closed to visitors.

of 40.23 m. These round minarets have octagonal bases; their face joints are countersunk and they are crowned with eight-windowed cupolas. Aldous Huxley thought they were the ugliest structures ever erected by human hands, but there are few who would agree with him. The massive plinth and the detached, towering minarets accentuate to perfection the delicate femininity of the tomb.

Leopold von Orlich, a German mercenary who visited the Taj Mahal in 1845, wrote of the minarets:

. . . they have within a winding staircase of

that point I have seen not only the rising and setting of the sun, but also the fairy place illuminated by the light of the moon. At these times the most solemn silence prevails; the air is more filled than ever with the aromatic perfume of the flowers, and a magic glow is shed over the wondrous building.

Within the tomb, the two-storeyed structure of the exterior is repeated and the layout is as symmetrical. The large central octagonal hall is like a jewel within a jewel and strangely fragile, though the soffit of the dome rises to 24.35 m.

The actual tombs of Shah Jahan and Mumtaz Mahal are placed in a crypt exactly beneath the cenotaphs, of which they are an exact replica.

162 steps, which leads to the very summit. . . . The finest prospect is from the upper gallery of the south-east minaret, and from

Facing page: *The cenotaphs of Mumtaz Mahal and Shah Jahan in the upper chamber of the Taj are encircled by a marble screen. All the sides of the monument except the south entrance are also enclosed with delicately perforated marble screens filled with translucent glass, so that a subdued filtered light invests the place. Adding to this diffused natural glow is the light that streams down from the Egyptian lamp that hangs from the ceiling, presented in 1909 by Lord Curzon.*

Here an echo "floats and soars overhead in a long delicious undulation, fading away so slowly that you hear it even after it is silent." On the four sides of this hall are four rectangular rooms, while at the corners are four octagonal rooms, all connected by a corridor. On the ground floor, the main hall is linked to the corner rooms by radiating passages. All the sides, except the south facing entrance, have been closed with translucent glass. The screens in the upper storeys as well as on the exterior have the same glass, allowing a very dim light to penetrate indoors. The only artificial light within is from the glow of the candles that are lit on the cenotaphs and from the brass lamp that hangs from the centre of the domed roof. This lamp was presented by Lord Curzon in 1909. He had taken great pains to find an appropriate design, and eventually had it fashioned in Egypt, after a similar lamp that adorned a mosque in Cairo.

In the heart of the main hall, perfectly in line with the central axis of the entire complex, is the cenotaph of Mumtaz Mahal. The marble is exquisitely translucent, the floral inlay so fine that it calls for a delicate touch. On the cenotaph is inscribed: "Those who say Allah is

On the slab over her husband there are no passages from the Koran; merely mosaic work of flowers, with his name, and the date of his death. I asked some of the learned Mohammedan attendants the cause of this difference; and was told that Shah Jahan had himself designed the slab over his wife, and saw no harm in inscribing the words of God upon it, but the slab over himself was designed by his more pious son Aurangzeb, who did not think it right to place these holy words upon a stone which the foot of men might some day touch, though the stones covered the remains of his own father . . .

A latticed octagonal screen of white marble, eight feet high, encloses the cenotaphs of Mumtaz Mahal and Shah Jahan. The finest stones are said to have been used for the pietra dura *inlay work on the screen.*

our God, shalt approach near unto the Divine presence." Below it is the epitaph: "Here lies Arjumand Bano Begum called Mumtaz Mahal who died in 1040 Hijri." Other verses from the Koran grace this cenotaph, but not that of Shah Jahan's, whose epitaph reads: "The sacred sepulchre of His Most Exalted Majesty, Dweller of Paradise, the Second Lord of Constellation, the King Shah Jahan, may his mausoleum ever flourish, 1706 Hijri." Colonel Sleeman, after visiting the Taj Mahal in 1844, offers an explanation for the absence of any scriptural verses on Shah Jahan's tomb.

Over the cenotaph of Mumtaz Mahal is a slate and over that of Shah Jahan is an inkwell, for it was believed that a man would write the desires of his soul on the heart of the woman, and she would fulfil them in heaven as she had done on earth.

Mumtaz Mahal's cenotaph was once encircled with a gold, jewelled rail. Fear of vandalism made Shah Jahan replace it with an exquisitely carved octagonal marble screen. Single slabs of marble have been carved in floral patterns, resulting in the finest filigree. The screen is bordered with inlaid arabesque of a quality that matches the work on the cenotaphs.

The French novelist, Pierre Loti, who visited the Taj Mahal in 1903, was especially charmed by this screen. He writes:

The wonder of wonders is the white grille that stands in the centre of the translucent hall and encloses the tomb of the Sultana. It is made of plaques of marble placed upright, so finely worked that it might be thought they were carved in ivory. On each marble upright, and each stud, with which these fretted marble plaques are surrounded, little garlands of tulips, fuschias and immortelles are worked in mosaics of turquoise, topaz, porphyry or lapis lazuli.

The arabesque inlay, the Koranic inscriptions and the *bas-relief* on the dados have a quiet elegance about them. They are ornate and striking, yet they do not distract from the focal point of the room which is the cenotaph of Mumtaz Mahal, and off-centre that of Shah Jahan.

These cenotaphs, however, are only illusory; the real graves are in a dark, airless crypt, directly below. As one enters the tomb, there are steps leading down to this crypt. The sepulchres here are replicas of the cenotaphs above, but their quality is visibly inferior. At one time, they were, if anything, more lavish then their counterparts, and encrusted with rare jewels. But they suffered at the hands of plunderers and today we see their restored version. The marble is not of similar quality and the inlay work not as smooth to the touch.

The tomb has a series of basement chambers, interconnected with corridors. Two staircases on the northern side of the sandstone plinth lead down to these chambers, but the entrance doors have been closed for over a century.

For all its resemblance to a jewel, the ornamentation of the Taj Mahal is very quiet. Unlike the tomb of Itmad-ud-Daulah which is over decorated, in the Taj Mahal the architect has discovered the beauty of marble itself, and designed "the most stainless mass of marble the world has ever seen." There is a preponderance of plain white surfaces that exude their own light. Even where there is ornamentation—in the inlay work, for instance—it is set against an adequate area of plain marble, so that both the marble and the jewelled inlay present their most beautiful aspects.

Subtle details have not missed the eye of the artisan. For example, the semi-octagonal pilasters are inlaid with yellow and black marble in the form of horizontal chevrons, creating the illusion that the edges are fluted. On the borders of the dados that flank these

The arch in the marble screen enclosing the cenotaphs. Mumtaz Mahal's illuminated sepulchre lies at the centre, immediately below the point of the dome. **Following pages 58-59:** *The cenotaph of Shah Jahan, which lies off-centre, is bigger and more ornate, as befits an emperor and in conformity with Islamic tradition.*

pilasters the chevron motif is repeated. But here the chevrons are vertical, and this quiet variation in line is pleasing to the eye.

The bordered dado panels seen throughout the tomb were first used at Akbar's tomb in Sikandra. There, they were outlined with black marble and set in red sandstone. The form was undoubtedly inspired by contemporary miniature paintings. Miniatures were mounted with finely painted *hashiyas* or borders in conventional floral patterns. There were special painters for this minutely exquisite work, which was considered an art in itself. These borders in turn were reminiscent of the arabesque scrolls of Persian art.

In the Agra Fort the dado panels are conventionalized but more refined than at

the cenotaphs, the borders of the marble screen and dado panels and the spandrels of the arches. The motif is arabesque, which is based fundamentally on geometric principles with repetitive and reciprocal curved lines. However, while the order imposed by a geometric pattern has been maintained in the carving, the artists have also beautifully expressed the sweetness of flowing outlines. Into these carved surfaces were placed jewels from the world over. Sometimes, a single flower is composed of as many as forty-eight pieces of precious and semiprecious stones to achieve the desired tonal variations. In deep,

Left: A carved floral panel on sandstone adorning the mosque on the left of the Taj.
Right: Intricate motifs in inlay work on white marble.

Sikandra. In the Taj Mahal the form reaches its height. Here, the *bas-relief* is not cramped and the inlaid borders are carefully distributed in the interior hall, the surrounding chambers and the exterior portals. The *bas-relief* is in floral patterns. From the mouth of a vase arises a spray of slender twigs, bearing beautiful flowers and buds which hang symmetrically on all sides, covering the central space of the dado between the inlaid borders. This graceful relief motif combines delicately with the coloured, inlaid border.

The inlay work on the Taj Mahal is seen on

rich earth colours they are at once luminous and restrained. On the spandrels the inlaid arabesque is more spaced out, more flowing, like an ornate embroidery. On the parapets, the cenotaphs and the border of the dados and marble screen, the pattern is more defined, geometric and contained, like a closely woven border. And so finely finished is the work that it feels more like silk than stone and marble. This, too, is reminiscent of miniatures.

"In these delicate patterns of precious stones," writes Percy Brown, "there is much that is reminiscent of the contemporary art of the painter. For the same motifs may be seen in the designs in the inlaid alabaster as on the flowered borders of the miniatures . . . in technique only do the two crafts differ, in the one the effects were obtained by coloured stones, in the other by pigments and burnished gold."

Yes, Shah Jahan surely had his chaste and exquisite bride of nineteen years in mind when he planned the Taj Mahal. The finished mausoleum was entirely to his satisfaction, and it expressed his feelings eloquently. Down the centuries it has been rumoured that he was so pleased with the result that he had the hands of

view, absorbing its strange silence, delighting in the landscape and the play of light on the marble. When they leave, they are haunted by the image of Taj Mahal, and wonder if what they have just seen is a reality in stone and marble or a fleeting vision of pure beauty.

Every visit to the Taj Mahal is a new and deeply enriching personal experience. Indeed, mere words or even superlatives are unequal to the taste of describing its incomparable beauty. As V.W. Stevens opined, "The man who should describe the Taj must own genius equal to his who built it."

The Taj Mahal as viewed from the corner tower of the Jamaat Khana.

the chief artisans chopped off, so that they could never duplicate the Taj Mahal. There is no evidence to prove this, as there is no doubt also that a second Taj Mahal can never be built.

For over three centuries people have visited the mausoleum. Some rush in hordes through the gateway, down the garden, around the cenotaphs and back to the garden to picnic on its lawns. Some see it only through the eyes of the camera. But there are many who pause, overwhelmed, at the gateway. They spend hours at the mausoleum, savouring its every

Even so, the lasting impression almost invariably is of the monument's ethereal magnificence and timeless harmony of proportion. As a whole, the Taj Mahal must be seen as a composite creation in eternal communion with the delicate interplay of three integrally related elements—the environment, in which river and sky are the main components, the 'charbagh' and the tomb itself. The harmonies of form and environment pulsating in companionship over time immemorial are perhaps the supreme achievement of the Taj Mahal.

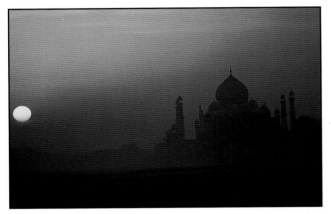

Glimpses of the Taj amidst the morning mist.

The silhouette acquires a soft ephemeral glimmer with the approach of dusk.

In light and shade.

In the soft rays of the morning sun.

THROUGH THE EYE OF THE BEHOLDER

In the last 300 years many have been so moved by the Taj Mahal that they have recorded their impressions at length. Some have described what they found most beautiful about the mausoleum; others have revealed the various activities that took place there.

To Shah Jahan it was a sacred ground, a precious memorial to a loved one. After his death, and at least till the end of Aurangzeb's reign, the monument continued to be held sacred. But as later travelogues reveal it was not always to be so.

The French traveller, Francois Bernier, visited the Taj Mahal during Aurangzeb's reign in 1670. He wrote of it in a letter to his patron, Jean Baptiste Colbert, the dreaded finance minister of Louis XIV of France:

The building I am speaking of is of a different and peculiar kind; but not without something pleasing in its whimsical structure; and in my opinion it well deserves a place in our books of architecture. It consists almost wholly of arches upon arches, and galleries upon galleries disposed and contrived in an hundred different ways. Nevertheless the edifice has a magnificent appearance, and is conceived and executed effactually. Nothing offends the eye; on the contrary, it is delighted with every part, and never tired with looking. The last time I visited Tage Mehale's mausoleum I was in the company of a French merchant (Tavernier) who, as well as myself, thought that this extraordinary fabric could not be sufficiently admired. I did not venture to express my opinion, fearing that my taste might have become corrupted by my long residence in the Indies; and as my companion was come recently from France, it was quite a relief to my mind to hear him say that he had seen nothing in Europe so bold and majestic.

There the Koran is continually read with apparent devotion in respectful memory of Tage Mehale by certain Mullahs kept in the mausoleum for that purpose. . . .

Everywhere are seen the jasper, and jachen, or jade, as well as other stones similar to those that enrich the walls of the Grand Duke's chapel at Florence, and several more of great value and rarity set in an endless variety of modes, mixed and encased in the slabs of marble which face the body of the wall. Even the squares of white and black marble which compose the pavement are inlaid with these precious stones in the most beautiful and delicate manner imaginable. Under the dome is a small chamber, wherein is enclosed the tomb of Tage Mehale. It is opened with much ceremony once a year, and once only; and as no Christian is admitted within, lest its sanctity should be profaned, I have not seen the interior, but I understand that nothing can be conceived more rich and magnificent.

It only remains to draw your attention to a walk or terrace, nearly five-and-twenty paces in breadth and rather more in height, which runs from the dome to the extremity of the garden. From this terrace are seen the Gemna flowing below, a large expanse of luxuriant gardens, a part of the city of Agra, the fortress, and all the fine residences of the Omrahs erected on the banks of the river. When I add that this terrace extends almost the whole length of one side of the garden, I leave you to judge whether I had not sufficient ground for asserting that the mausoleum of Tage Mehale is an astonishing work. It is possible I may have imbibed an Indian taste; but I decidedly think that this monument deserves much more to be numbered among the wonders of the world than the pyramids of Egypt, those unshapen masses which when I had seen them twice yielded me no satisfaction . . . (*Travels in the Mogul Empire*, 1670.)

Six years later Jean Baptise Tavernier again visited the mausoleum which he had seen frequently during its construction with his friend Bernier. Yes, Aurangzeb was taking

The translucent marble changes colour with the changing quality of light.

Reflecting as many moods as the phases of the day.

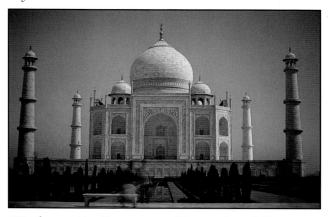

Utterly captivating on a shimmering full moon night.

Mirrored in the central waterway.

special care, for Tavernier writes:

> . . . the Begum is interred under a vault which is beneath the first platform. The same changes which are made below in this subterranean place are made around the tomb, for from time to time they change the carpet, chandeliers, and other ornaments of that kind, and there are always there some Mollahs to pray.

A hundred years later the scene at the Taj Mahal had changed. So had the Moghul Empire under the hands of successive

mullahs, it seems, had stopped praying there.

In 1783, the British painter Hodges visited the Taj Mahal and made the first known painting of this mausoleum. He found the garden in "tolerable repair" but the tomb itself, he says, "appears like a most perfect pearl on an azure ground. The effect is such, I confess, I never experienced from any work of art."

Visitors, both Indian and foreign, continued to frequent the Taj Mahal. Thomas Daniell, another British painter, testified to this in 1789:

> The Taj Mahal has always been considered

The Taj Mahal, —always illusory and ethereal—in the incandescent glow of dusk or dawn.

weaklings. Not that the mausoleum had lost its beauty, for it was to be a source of much inspiration to British painters. But the

Facing page: *View of the Taj from across the waters of the Jamuna. On either side of the Taj are two identical red sandstone structures each topped by three marble domes. The two buildings are locally also called sawal or query and jawab or response. The design of the buildings echoes the Taj in muted fashion, replicating its arches and domes. The two structures were built essentially to provide symmetry to the main monument.*

as the first example of Mohammedan architecture in India, and consequently, being a spectacle of the highest celebrity, is visited by persons of all ranks and from all parts. The high admiration is however, not confined to the partial eye of the native Indian; it is beheld with no less wonder and delight by those who have seen the productions of art in various parts of the globe.

But by the turn of the century the attitude to Indian art and architecture had changed.

An early morning view of the mausoleum, as the sun rises over yet another day. Eternal in the sands of time, it stands as witness, in silent majesty, to the passage of centuries.

Bentinck, the first Governor-General of India (1928-33), had planned to demolish several monuments in Delhi and Agra and remove their facades, to be shipped and sold to the gentry in England. Some pavilions at the Agra Fort fell victim to this bizarre plan. Even the Taj Mahal was to be dismantled, but word of the failure to sell the marble in London arrived in time.

By the nineteenth century all sanctity and quiet had been removed from the Taj Mahal. The beautiful memorial had been turned into a pleasure resort; in its gardens, Englishmen met their lovers, on its terrace they danced, while the mosque and the *jawab* were rented out to honeymooners. In 1844 the well-known Colonel Sleeman gave the following account:

For five and twenty years of my life had I been looking forward to the sight now before me. Of no building on earth had I heard so much as of this, which contains the remains of the Emperor Shah Jahan and his wife . . . and from the first sight of the dome and minarets on the distant horizon, to the last glance back from my tent-ropes to the magnificent gateway that forms the entrance from our camp to the quadrangle in which they stand, I can truly say that everything surpassed my expectations. I at first thought the dome formed too large a portion of the whole building; that its neck was too long and too much exposed; and that the minarets were too plain in their design; but after going repeatedly over every part, and examining the *tout ensemble* from all possible positions, and in all possible lights, from that of the full moon at midnight in a cloudless sky, to that of the noon-day sun, the mind seemed to repose in the calm persuasion that there was an entire harmony of parts, a faultless congregation of architectural beauties, on which it could dwell forever without fatigue.
I went on from part to part in the expectation that I must by-and-by come to something that would disappoint me; but no, the emotion which one feels at first is never impaired: on the contrary, it goes on improving from the first *coup d'oeil* of the dome in the distance, to the minute inspection of the last flower upon the screen around the tomb. One returns and returns to it with undiminished pleasure; and though at every return one's attention to the smaller parts becomes less and less, the pleasure which he derives from the contemplation of the greater, and of the whole collectively, seems to increase; and he leaves it with a feeling of regret, that he could not have it all his life within his reach; and of the assurance that the image of what he has seen can never be obliterated from his mind . . . the fountains are made to play almost every evening when the gardens are frequented by the European gentlemen and ladies of the station, and by natives of all religious sects. . . . We were encamped upon a fine green sward outside the entrance to the south, in a kind of large court, enclosed by a high cloistered wall, in which all our attendants and followers found shelter. Colonel and Mrs King, and some other gentlemen were encamped in the same place, and for the same purpose; and we had a very agreeable party. The band of our friend Major Godby's regiment played sometimes in the evening upon the terrace of the Taj; but of all the complicated music ever heard upon earth, that of a flute blown gently in the vault below, where the remains of the Emperor and his consort repose, as the sound rises to the dome amidst . . . arched alcoves around, and descends in heavenly reverberations upon those who sit or recline upon the cenotaphs above the vault, is perhaps the finest to an inartificial ear. We feel as if it were from heaven . . . (W. H. Sleeman, *Rambles and Recollections of an Indian Official*, 1844.)

Sleeman's wife did not write at length of her reactions, but she was nonetheless expressive in her brevity. "I cannot tell you what I think," she wrote to a friend, "for I know not how to criticize such a building, but I can tell you what I feel. I would die tomorrow to have such another over me."

Among the hundreds of European mercenaries who sought employment in India in the nineteenth century was a German, Leopold von Orlich. He came to Agra a year after Sleeman, and records the desecration of the mausoleum. Some care, however, was being taken, which he notes:

> The garden is always filled with fragrant flowers, and is intended to represent eternal spring; and the wanderer finds protection against the scorching rays of the sun, under the shade of the tamarind, banyan, fig, and mango trees . . .
> From the left side of the principal entrance, sacrilegious hands had stolen a few of the most valuable stones out of the mosaic; but the British government has had the place repaired under the direction of Captain Boileau, and paid 3000 rupees for the restoration of these few arabesques! Keepers and gardeners are now appointed, and on Sundays the fountains play, and hundreds of people visit the spot . . .
> The Jumna meanders, like a stream of silver, through the verdant landscape; the ruins of places and sepulchres cast a mysterious shade; and Agra, with its minarets and elegant marble palaces in the boldly rising citadel, seems to be shrouded in a mystic veil, under which the numerous lights of the strand and the bazaars sparkle like little stars. (Leopard von Orlich, *Travels in India*, 1845.)

What a perfectly oriental setting. No wonder, then, that it became increasingly popular as a pleasure resort. So much so that by 1855 a British hotel, Beaumont, opened at Agra. It provided "refreshing and clean accommodation and skilled natives expert at carving the following items for those who care to buy: inkstands, black stone serpents, paper cutters and marble Taj Mahals."

The American novelist, Bayard Taylor, wrote about the Taj Mahal:

> The vault was filled with the odours of rose, jasmine, and sandal-wood, the precious attars of which are sprinkled upon the tomb. Wreaths of beautiful flowers lay upon it, or withered around its base. The Taj truly is . . .

a poem. It is not only a pure architectural type, but also a creation which satisfies the imagination, because its characteristic is Beauty. Did you ever build a Castle in the Air? Here is one, brought down to earth, and fixed for the wonder of ages; yet so light it seems, so airy, and when seen from a distance, so like a fabric of mist and sunbeams . . . that, even after you have touched it, and climbed to its summit, you almost doubt its reality . . .

Obviously there was also the expected criticism by the 'natives' about the way the Taj Mahal was being misused. A guidebook of 1872 records:

> It would certainly be more in character if no festivities ever disturbed the repose of a place set aside for sacred memories; but as long as the natives hold constant fairs in the enclosure and throw orange peels and other debris about the whole place it is perhaps somewhat hypocritical to object to a few Englishmen refreshing themselves in a remote corner.

Yes, the garden seemed an ideal place for the British soldier wanting to enjoy his drink. Not all soldiers, however, were oblivious to the beauty of the mausoleum. In 1873, Robert Ogden Tyler, an American soldier, wrote, "See by the moonlight the darker inlaid work and the discolouration disappear, and all is pure white. The lines and tracery are softened and blended, and its seems so delicate and intangible that one would hardly be surprised if at some moment it should melt like a cloud into thin air."

A variety of people visited the Taj Mahal and the last century too had its share of the proverbial tourist. In 1887, Rudyard Kipling wrote of one such tourist in his book, *From Sea to Sea*:

> a man who had . . . read a great deal too much about Taj, its designs and proportions, to have seen execrable pictures of it at the Simla Fine Arts Exhibition, to have had its praises sung by superior and travelled

friends till the brain loathed the repetition of the word.

. . . then as the train sped forward, and the mists shifted and the sun shone upon the mists, the Taj took a hundred new shapes, each perfect and each beyond description. It was the Ivory Gate through which all dreams come true . . . it seemed the embodiment of all things pure, all things holy and all things unhappy. That was the mystery of the building. It may be that the mists wrought the witchery, and that the Taj seen in the dry sunlight is only, as guidebooks say, a noble structure. The Englishman could not tell, and

died in the building, used up like cattle. And in the face of this sorrow the Taj flushed in the sunlight and was beautiful, after the beauty of a woman who has done no wrong.

Fortunately, by the turn of the century, there was once again a growing interest in Indian art and architecture. This, coupled with the personal interest taken by Lord Curzon, the new Governor-General, saved the Taj Mahal, and indeed several other ancient monuments all over the country, from total neglect. He had monuments painstakingly restored; palaces were no longer used as kitchens or barracks for

From a distance, the Taj Mahal is overpowering in its beauty, but not in its size. But as one draws closer the mausoleum looms larger and larger, till it finally dominates the landscape.

has made a vow that he will never go nearer the spot, for fear of breaking the charm of the unearthly pavilions.

It may be, too, that each must view the Taj for himself, with his own eyes, working out his own interpretation of the sight. It is certain that no man in cold blood and colder ink set down his impressions if he has been in the least moved. To the one who watched and wondered that November morning the thing seemed full of sorrow—the sorrow of the man who built it for the woman he loved, and the sorrow of the workmen who

soldiers, mausoleums were no longer pleasure resorts, to mention just a few misuses the ancient edifices had suffered.

The Taj Mahal that Lord Curzon first saw had become a dilapidated structure with an overgrown garden. The precious stones had been removed by idlers and thieves, the water channels were choked with neglect and there were cracks in the marble. All this was attended to. Special artisans were trained to replace the inlay work; water channels were cleared, the marble repaired and polished, and the garden manicured. As Lord Curzon himself remarked: "At an early date, when picnic parties were held in the garden of the Taj, it was not an uncommon thing for the revellers to arm themselves with hammer and chisel, with which they whiled away the afternoon by chipping out fragments of agate and cornelian from the cenotaphs of the Emperor and his lamented Queen."

Mercifully, this was never to happen again. Lord Curzon was especially enamoured of the Taj Mahal, and it was with a sense of great pleasure that he was able to write that the mausoleum was

. . . no longer approached through dust wastes and squalid bazaars. A beautiful park takes their place and the group of mosques and tombs, the arcaded streets and the grassy courts that precede the buildings, are once more nearly as possible what they were when completed by the masons of Shah Jahan. Every building in the garden enclosure of the Taj has been scrupulously repaired, and the discovery of old plans has enabled us to restore the water channels and flower beds in the garden more exactly to their original state.

In a speech from the terrace of the Taj Mahal, Lord Curzon said: "The central dome of the Taj rises like some vast exhalation into the thin air, and on the other side the red rampart of the Fort stands like a crimson barricade against the sky . . . If I had never done anything else in India, I have written my name here, and the letters are a living joy."

Today, once again, the Taj Mahal is cherished and preserved, as indeed the Emperor of the World had meant it to be.

Shah Jahan's own composition in praise of the Taj is found in the *Badshah Nama*:

How excellent the sepulchre of the lady of Bilqis's fame
That a cradle for the body of the Princess of the World became.
Like the garden of heaven a brilliant spot.
Full of fragrance like paradise fraught with ambergris.
In the breath of its court perfumes from the nose-gay of sweetheart rise,
The nymps of paradise use their eye-lids for cleaning its threshold.
Its walls and gates glitter with gems,
The air is there fresh and delightlful like brilliancy of pearl.
The architect of this sacred edifice
Brought water for it from the fountain if grace.
On this sacred edifice of high renown
Showers of mercy are ever pouring.
Should guilt seek asylum here,
Like one pardoned, he becomes free from sin.
Should a sinner make his way to this mansion,
All his past sins are sure to be washed away.
The sight of this mansion creates sorrowing sighs
And makes sun and moon shed tears from their eyes.
In this world this edifice has been made
To display thereby the Creator's glory.

Rabindranath Tagore echoed the feelings of its admirers when he wrote:

You knew, Shah Jahan, life and youth, wealth and glory, they all drift away in the current of time. You strove, therefore, to perpetuate only the sorrow of your heart. Kingly power, stern as thunder, may sink into sleep like the glowing embers of the setting sun . . . Let the splendour of diamond, pearl and ruby vanish like the magic shimmer of the rainbow. Only let this one teardrop, this Taj Mahal, glisten spotlessly bright on the cheek of time, forever and ever.

Following pages 72-73: *Full view of the Taj from across the river—as much of a tribute to its creator as to the eternal love and beauty it was destined to immortalize. When Shah Jahan wanted to visit the Taj Mahal, he would come down the Jamuna on the royal barge from his palace in the Agra Fort. The river Jamuna had been diverted to the foot of the foundations before the construction of the complex was begun, so that the vista from the completed tomb would be improved.*

71

FATEHPUR SIKRI

Akbar's greatest architectural achievement was his dream city atop the ridge at Sikri, built in grateful thanksgiving to the Sufi saint, Shaikh Salim Chisti, whose blessings, the emperor believed, had been instrumental in enriching his life with three sons. He gave the name Salim (after the saint) to his first son, born in 1569, and resolved to create an entirely new capital city at Sikri in his honour.

Though Agra continued to remain the military stronghold, the new capital at Sikri was to emerge as its cultural and administrative twin for the next fifteen years. The shaikh had his hermitage on a low hill consisting of hard red sandstone, a perfectly durable material for construction. Over the next nine years, a new city was literally raised from the rock beneath the Sikri hill. In 1574, Akbar named it "Fatehpur," denoting a place of victory, after his conquest of the south, and hence the new complex came to be known as Fatehpur Sikri.

Akbar, the creator of this once bustling red sandstone city, is himself believed to have devised the layout of the complex. He made skilful use of the jagged features of the Aravalli hills and the asymmetries of the natural setting. In this he was assisted by the finest talent in the empire. Akbar is said to have thrown himself into the project with his customary zeal, often working alongside the builders, as recorded by Monserrate.

Facing page: The central sandstone pillar of the Diwan-i-Khas or Hall of Private Audience at Fatehpur Sikri. Featuring intricately carved brackets, it supports the platform seat of the emperor in the centre, as well as the four bridges that radiate from it to the balconies on the sides. A marvel as a work of craftsmanship, its purpose, it is believed, was to provide seclusion for discussions between the emperor and his "nine jewels" (navratans)—Tansen, Birbal, Todar Mal, Abul Fazl, Bhagwantdas, Abdul Rahim, Mansingh, among others—seated in the balconies.

The place of honour on the summit of the hill was given to the tomb of Salim Chisti, after he died in 1574. The exquisite shrine built for him was originally executed in the red sandstone of Fatehpur and later chastely veneered with white marble by Akbar's grandson, Shah Jahan, who had a passionate attachment to marble. The shrine's beauty is enhanced by its being placed in a setting of subdued rock and red sandstone, not quite in the centre of the vast, surrounding courtyard. Surrounded by stone-pierced screens, the cenotaph chamber is decorated with lapis-lazuli, mother-of-pearl and topaz. The western end of the courtyard is occupied by the Jami Masjid, said to be one of the largest and finest mosques in India. The approach is through a triumphal gateway, the Buland Darwaza or Portal of Victory, which the emperor got constructed after his return from his successful campaign in the Deccan. Completed in 1576, the Buland Darwaza is reached by a flight of steps rising forty feet high and positioned along the flank of the hill. The imposing gateway is visible for miles around, its massive contours softened by the filigree of cupolas and *chattris* (kiosks) which define the skyline.

East of the courtyard, and a little lower on the hill, in modest submission as it were, lies what remains of the imperial complex, interspersed with intricate casket-like buildings featuring elaborately carved stone ornamentation, crisp and unweathered to this day. A distinctive feature of Fatehpur Sikri is that the architectural features and decorative motifs adorning the buildings are derived from both Hindu and Islamic traditions, providing evidence of Akbar's aspiration for the emergence of a composite culture. In this sense, Fatehpur Sikri is Akbar's very own capital. In keeping with Islamic tradition, the imperial complex consisted of three distinct groups—the palaces, the seraglio and the royal offices—each closely interrelated. The three groups were aligned with the Jami Masjid, slightly athwart the axis of the ridge. However, the present categorization of the various functions of each building is more guesswork than documented fact.

The focus of the town-plan was the royal complex. This included the Khana-i-Khas (Abode of Fortune) or the imperial residence, made up of a room on the floor above, the Khwabgah (or royal bedroom), and the emperor's library on the ground floor which has niches carved in it for storing books. The other room on the ground floor was used by the emperor to consult with his ministers and is also called the *diwan-i-khas*.

which, barring pairs, are alike. Overlooking the seraglio, the Panch Mahal was originally provided with delicately carved stone screens concealing the royal ladies, for whom it was intended, from public view while allowing them to observe functions. Though Persian in concept, it is entirely Indian in execution.

At the western end is the palace known as Birbal Mahal, named after Akbar's boon companion. The name appears to be a clear misnomer since the palace formed an integral part of Akbar's harem complex. Birbal Mahal occupies the most prized position of all the palaces in Fatehpur. Made of sandstone, it is

The shrine of Shaikh Salim Chisti at Fatehpur Sikri. Originally executed in red sandstone, the shrine was faced with white marble by Akbar's grandson, Shah Jahan.

The Anup Talao (Peerless Pool) which lies in front of the royal residence is elaborately adorned with floral designs alternating with arabesques. The elegant pavilion adjoining Anup Talao, which displays the finest carvings in Fatehpur, was the residence of Ruqiah Sultana Begam, Akbar's chief consort.

The most striking amongst the palace buildings is the 5-tiered Panch Mahal. It consists of five pillared floors, each diminishing in size up to a small pavilion at the apex, giving it the appearance of an irregular open pyramid. It is made of 176 pillars, no two of

richly carved in the Hindu tradition, and is reputed to be one of Fatehpur Sikri's most beautiful residential building.

Southwest of the Sunehra Makan or Golden House, which is believed to have been the residence of Akbar's Christian wife, Mariam Zamani, is Jodha Bai's Mahal. Jodha Bai, Akbar's Hindu wife and the daughter of the Raja of Amber, lived in the palace whose blue-tiled rectangular roof still retains much of its original brilliance.

Adjoining Jodha Bai's Mahal is the Hawa Mahal, or Palace of Breezes, a screened first-floor pavilion for the enjoyment of the ladies. From here they could descend along screened passages to Hathi Pol gate to enjoy the cool waters of Sikri lake. The lake has long since been drained and taken over for cultivation.

Among the royal offices, the Diwan-i-Khas (Hall of Private Audience) and the Diwan-i-Am (Hall of Public Audience) are the two most noteworthy buildings.

The Diwan-i-Khas is a marvellous work of craftsmanship. It is one large, high room, in the centre of which is a sturdy sandstone pillar connected at the top to the four corners by finely carved brackets, The pillar that holds up a raised circular platform is called the Throne Pillar, where the emperor is said to have sat. It is believed that the more secluded confines of the Diwan-i-Khas were used by Akbar for confidential discussions on matters of state.

The Diwan-i-Am was the focal point of the imperial complex. It is a vast assembly hall, held up by immense, slender columns, where Akbar is believed to have disbursed justice to his subjects. Its aura of dignity and amplitude was heightened by a majestic lantern suspended from a great height in front of the entrance.

Further west of the Diwan-i-Am is the main courtyard in the palace complex, where a *pachisi* (chess) board is embedded in the stone floor with a roughly fashioned stone seat in the centre. This is where Akbar is believed to have seated himself, while playing a variant of ludo with live slave girls. Nearby is the building of the Ankh Michauli, which was actually a treasury. It is lined with recesses which were covered with sliding slabs of stone, where gold and silver coins are believed to have been stored.

Akbar is recorded to have made a daily appearance at dawn at a *jharoka* or window in the southern wall of the Khana-i-Khas below his Khwabgah for his first informal *darshan* of the day. This special mode of presenting himself was an old Hindu custom adopted by Akbar as a living compact with the people of his empire. A little later in the day, he would proceed to the Diwan-i-Am, passing the Anup Talao on the way, to the accompaniment of drum-beats emanating from the Naqqar Khana.

Fatehpur Sikri served as Akbar's imperial capital till 1556, when Akbar left it to crush an incipient rebellion in the Punjab and thereafter returned towards the end of his reign in 1598, to Agra, never again to Fatehpur Sikri.

Today, Fatehpur Sikri rests in tranquil serenity, haunted by the glories of the past. It is a perfectly preserved ghost town and has been declared a World Heritage Monument. What remains in a perfect state even today is the imperial complex, the outer wall, the mosque and the tomb. Though the mosque appears to be no longer in use, the shrine of Chisti commands the same devotion as do the most renowned shrines all over India. It was in

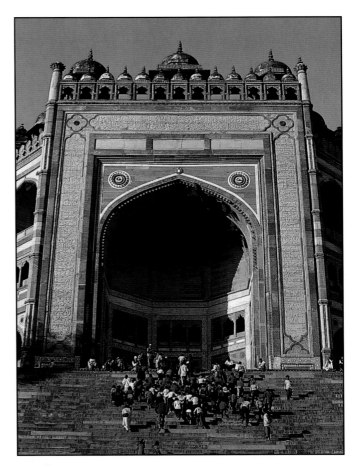

The Buland Darwaza or Mighty Portal at Fatehpur Sikri, a victory gate rising 176 feet from the ground, that Akbar built to commemorate his successful campaign in the Deccan. **Following pages 78-79:** *A misty view of the Taj on a winter morning through arches from a spot to its east.*

Fatehpur Sikri that Akbar had devised the eclectic religious faith called Din-i-illahi, but like the city itself, the new spirit did not last beyond its founder.

© This edition Roli & Janssen BV 2006
Seventh impression

ISBN: 81-7437-057-9

Published in India by Roli Books
in arrangement with Roli & Janssen BV
M-75 Greater Kailash, II Market, New Delhi 110 048, India.
Phone: ++91-11-29212271, 29212782; Fax: ++91-11-29217185
E-mail: roli@vsnl.com; Website: rolibooks.com

Text: Shalini Saran
Revised Text: Chaitali Basu
Text Editor: Bela Butalia
Concept and Design: Roli CAD Centre

Photocredits:

Ashok Dilwali, D. N. Dube,
Karoki Lewis, Pramod Kapoor

Printed and bound at
Star Standard Industries Pte. Ltd., Singapore